Building
Ailey

BY NATAN BIBLIOWICZ

Publisher
Natan Bibliowicz

Book design
Liana Zamora, Mitch Shostak/Shostak Studios, Inc.

All Illustrations unless otherwise noted
Natan Bibliowicz

Photography
Arch Photo

Contributors
Carolyn Iu
David Bibliowicz (illustrations)
Richard Balestrino
Robert Benchley
David Delp

Building Ailey is published by
Natan Bibliowicz
212-982-3633
e-mail: nb@ibarchitects.com

Iu+Bibliowicz Architects LLP
57 East 11 Street
New York, New York 10003
www.ibarchitects.com

Oceanic Graphic Printing
Printed in China

© 2008 by Natan Bibliowicz
ISBN: 978-0-9801240-0-2

The People That Built Ailey

A. Liss & Co.	Toilet accessories, lockers
Aegis Protective Services	Security services
Airflex Industrial Inc.	Metalwork
Albert Pearlman, Inc.	Painting and wallcovering
American Architectural Inc.	Metal and Glass
Athena Networks	Information technology and security
Atlantic-Heydt Corporation	Hoisting and Sidewalk shed
Atlantic Rolling Door	Overhead doors
Boro Associates, LLC	Spray fireproofing
Brevoort Construction Inc.	Concrete
Cast Con Stone Inc.	Precast concrete
Cerami & Associates, Inc.	Audio/visual
City View Blinds and Shades Co.	Window treatment
Cives Steel Co.	Structural steel and metal deck
Claudia Wagner	Legal advisor
Commercial Kitchen Design	Appliances
Consolidated Edison Co.	Power supply
Crystal Studios Photographers	Construction photography
Cushman & Wakefield, Inc.	Owner's real estate advisor
Design 360 Inc.	Graphic design
Development Consulting Services, Inc.	Zoning consultant
Eurotech Construction Corp.	Masonry and EIFS
Fire Systems, Inc.	Fire alarm
Fisher Dachs Associates	Theater consultant
Forest Electric Corp.	Electrical
FTL	Tensile structure consultant
Fujitec New York	Elevator
Garcia Marble and Tile, Inc.	Ceramic tile
Gilsanz Murray Steficek, LLP	Structural engineer
Hallen Welding Service, Inc.	Misc metal
Haywood-Berk Floor Company, Inc.	Isolated wood flooring
Henick-Lane, Inc.	HVAC
Herman Miller, Inc.	Furniture
Hirani Consulting, Inc.	Site safety
Hirani Engineering & Land Surveying, P.C.	Site safety
I. Weiss	Stage draperies
Industrial Acoustics Co., Incorporated	Operable partitions
Innovative Security Systems & Systems, Inc.	Security consultant
Irwing Telescopic Seating Co.	Telescoping Seating
Iu + Bibliowicz Architects, LLP	Architect
JAM Consultants, Inc.	Expediting and code consultant
Jaros Baum & Bolles	MEP engineer
John Civetta & Sons, Inc.	Excavation and foundation
Jones, Lang, LaSalle	Owner's representative
Knoll, Inc.	Furniture
Langan Engineering	Geotechnical engineer
Lastrada General Contracting	Site work
Linear Technologies	Telephone and data
M2L	Lounge furniture
Modernfold/Styles, Inc.	Movable walls
National Roofing Co.	Roofing and waterproofing
Newport Painting, Inc.	Painting
NYC Billionaires Construction Corp.	Carpentry/drywall/ceilings/hardware/hollow metal
NYC Department of Cultural Affairs	Public funding agency
NYC Department of Design and Construction	Public funding
New York City Department of Transportation	
Par Plumbing Co., Inc.	Plumbing
Patti Fireproofing Corp.	Spray fireproofing
Premier Fire Sprinkler	Fire protection
R&S Floor Covering & Interiors	Flooring, carpet, VCT, cork and linoleum
Robert Derector Telecommunications	Information technology consultant
Safeway Environment Corp	Abatement and demolition
Signs and Decal Corp.	Signs
Seasons Contracting Corp.	Adjacent building stabilization
Sopers Fabric Products LTD	Tensile structures
South Jersey Metal, Inc.	Appliances
Specialty Flooring Systems, Inc.	Terrazzo
SRG Construction Consulting Corp.	Ornamental meta and glasswork
Strang Electric Co., Inc.	Security
Tatco Installations, Inc.	Millwork
Testwell Laboratories, Inc.	Testing and inspection
Tishman Construction Corporation of New York	Construction managers
Van Deusen & Associates	Elevator consultant
Visionwall Corp.	Curtain wall, windows, and entrances
W. B. Wood	Furniture dealer
Wausau Windows and Wall Systems	Curtain-wall fabrication subcontractor
Whitestone Construction Corp.	Exterior Curtain wall

Dedication

To Tommy and David,
with all my love.

*Your reason and your passion are the rudder and the sails
of your seafaring soul.*

*If either your sails or your rudder be broken, you can but
toss and drift, or else be held at a standstill in mid-seas.*

*For reason, ruling alone, is a force confining; and passion,
unattended, is a flame that burns to its own destruction.*

*Therefore let your soul exalt your reason to the height
of passion, that it may sing;*

*And let it direct your passion with reason, that your passion
may live through its own daily resurrection, and like the
phoenix rise above its own ashes.*

—KAHLIL GIBRAN, *THE PROPHET*

"Part of the beauty of this building for me is how everyone became a part of it. Natan & Carolyn interviewed the staff, the school, as well as the first and second companies. It is a structure that represents the Ailey family. Helping to make a dream come true is a rare and humbling experience. Both Sandy and I are so proud to have been a part of helping our Ailey family create its permanent home and giving our extraordinary students and professionals the space they so richly deserve. Thanks to the Alvin Ailey American Dance Theater board, our donors, friends, the community, staff, and Carolyn and Natan. As Judith Jamison says, 'We have our Palace.'"

—JOAN WEILL, *chairman of the board,*
  Alvin Ailey American Dance Theater

Introduction

I've spent seven years with the Alvin Ailey American Dance Theater, not as a dancer but as its architect. My first encounter, when I visited Ailey's former dance studios on 211 West 61st Street, was one of fascination. I was confronted by the sights and sounds of classes taking place all around me—drums and piano being played, people yelling, and lots and lots of energy and sweat. The student dancers were everywhere —lying on the floor, stretching, sleeping, eating, studying. They were an obstacle course between the lobby and the offices where Carolyn Iu, my partner, and I would meet with Ailey officials.

This was an experience I never tired of. The first projects our firm, Iu + Bibliowicz Architects, did for Ailey were at its 61st Street facility and had to do with capturing space and making it more efficient. They needed so much but had so little to work with.

Soon, however, we started talking about long-term needs. If Ailey was to grow and prosper, it would need to create a dance building with the right amount of studio space and the right amount of support for all the dancers, from young students to those in the First Company.

We began to explore alternatives that would meet their needs. What would happen if

Ailey took possession of four floors in the building it was already occupying? We designed a dynamic facility that doubled the current space, adding much-needed studios and other support spaces.

This was all great, but it was just a dream. It required agreement from the landlord and the incentive of a good business deal. After failed negotiations and much thinking, the board of directors decided to look elsewhere. We worked with key members of the board to analyze potential options: move Ailey to the base floors of new residential or commercial ventures, build a stand-alone building, explore potential city-sponsored sites,

Equally rewarding was meeting the craftsmen working with us—the excavators, ironworkers, electricians, plumbers, and concrete contractors.

move downtown to Ground Zero, and so on.

After we had designed several buildings at different locations, the board decided the best and most logical location–the one that met all of Ailey's needs and hopes– was 405 West 55th Street, where the old WNET Theater was housed. We found it fateful that this was the site where Alvin Ailey was televised for the first time.

Now the excitement really began. Designing a building in New York City is an unusual opportunity. The emotional experience of seeing it getting built is difficult, if not impossible, to describe.

Knowing that a building that had been in existence for several decades was being torn down to make way for the building we designed was–quite selfishly– exhilarating. Carolyn and I visited the site to watch the progress. Our excitement

would increase as the subway approached our stop at 55th Street and Seventh Avenue. The walk to Ninth Avenue filled our stomachs with butterflies: it took too long! We couldn't wait to get there to see and hear the people at work on the site that was *our* site, the new home of the Alvin Ailey American Dance Theater.

Equally rewarding was meeting the people working with us—the excavators, ironworkers, electricians, plumbers, and concrete contractors. I watched them carefully as they made their individual contributions to the project. Their faces revealed their dedication, their expertise, their love of their trade. Meeting them, if only for a moment to exchange hellos and talk about their work, reflected the real nature of what we were all doing there. We were all building Ailey, a building dedicated exclusively to dance

and the largest building of its kind in the country.

I really wanted to connect with all of them. I wanted to tell them that this is the most important project in the whole world. They needed to make it perfect. Please, no mistakes.

We took photographs while they worked. We tried to

capture a moment in time, a piece of their soul, with our digital cameras. Later, from a vast array of photos, I would choose the one that touched me the most. That is how this book project began.

The next time we came by the site, I gave each worker a copy of their portrait as a token of gratitude for what they were doing. After we had done this a few times, some of the workers began to approach us and ask for their photograph to be taken.

The drawings— nearly 200 in all —were a way for me to express my satisfaction at seeing the project evolve from idea to reality. The building is now complete, and the dancers bring life to it every day. The people in the drawings helped make that possible, and I hope their sense of pride matches my own.

—NATAN BIBLIOWICZ

Groundbreaking
celebration

JUDITH JAMISON
Artistic director,
ALVIN AILEY AMERICAN
DANCE THEATER

Foreword

Alvin Ailey would have loved this building. For as long as I'd known him, he had wanted a permanent home for the company he founded, the Alvin Ailey American Dance Theater. Although we had flourished in several spaces over the decades, he saw clearly that we must have our own home. He wanted a sense of expanding possibilities for his company—a place to start from, a place to reach out from. He envisioned the entire community coming through the company's welcoming doors.

He did not live to see it happen. After his death in 1989, when I became the artistic director, I knew that it was imperative to make his dream become a reality. When Natan Bibliowicz, of the architectural firm Iu + Bibliowicz Architects, began working with us on plans for the new building, I wanted him to know what Mr. Ailey would have wanted and to understand what this new place would mean for the company.

Mr. Ailey founded the company based on the intersection of African-American cultural expression and the American modern dance tradition. But he truly loved all humanity.

He liked to meet all kinds of people, and he wanted to engage everyone he met as a person, not just as a dancer or student, not just a label. The crucial part of any enterprise in Mr. Ailey's mind was the human being: his building had to be a place of humanity, warmth, generosity, and openness.

Natan got it. He and his partner, Carolyn Iu, created not only a home for us but also a statement about American dance. The sunlight floods into the fifth-floor dance studios during the day; at night the same space appears to float, illuminated, in midair. From strategically placed glass walls and walkways we gaze down on classes in session or catch a glimpse of a tree in the rear courtyard. The height of the ceiling in the belowground black-box theater continually surprises me, as does the wonderful, ambient light even in the lower floors. The colors in the lobby, the curving shapes, are calm, strong, elegant, and full of Ailey energy.

Everywhere we turn there is evidence of our 50-year history, from the framed and wisely grouped posters and memorabilia on the walls to our future—the dancers of every age and level studying, rehearsing, talking, or even snoozing in a quiet corner. It is a welcoming place, not only for us but also for our neighbors; the community fills our space for evening and weekend extension programs. We are part of the city around us. Day and night, the building is alive.

Looking back, I am overwhelmed by what it took to make this happen. I remember how far we have come and how hard we worked. So many people generously helped make real the vision of a man who embodied generosity of heart and mind. Still, I had not realized just how enormous an undertaking this

> The crucial part of any enterprise, in Mr. Ailey's mind, was the human being: his building had to be a place of humanity, warmth, generosity, and openness.

would be: to raise the building, but also to inhabit it, to breathe life into it.

In October 2002 we broke ground at 405 West 55th Street for what was to be the Joan Weill Center for Dance. (I know it was more than coincidence that, of the number of possible sites for our new home, we settled on the spot of Mr. Ailey's first televised performance of *Revelations*—the old WNET broadcast studio.) Giant machines dug the foundation and raised the steel beams. Amid the unbelievable noise, workers applied their skills to cement, iron, wire, and wood.

Like any good architect, Natan is fascinated by the activity of building. I share his enthusiasm for construction sites. The sight of a hard hat reminds me of my father, who wore one on the job all his working life. I loved to visit the site, going up and down

in the cage elevator with a hard hat on my head, saying hello to everyone. Nicky, the foreman, would hold my hand as we carefully stepped down unfinished stairways. Nicky and Natan would say, "And this is the theater…" All I could see were beams! Of course, Natan could picture the finished space. Eventually, as the work progressed, I could see it, too.

Natan roamed through all the daily commotion photographing machines, walls, and people. I'd always thought that drawing was only the beginning stage for an architect, but for Natan the drawing never stopped. At night, at his home using his photos as a visual journal, he poured his reverence for the people and the process into hundreds of charcoal and pastel drawings.

The pictures chronicle not only the realization of his ideas in steel, glass, and concrete, but they also

honor what I like to think of as the dance theater's first residents: the builders.

The drawings remind me of some of the work of the New York realists John Sloan and George Bellows, showing urban people and places in gritty, black-and-white lithographs; the photography of the 1930s documenting the raising of the new 20th-century city; Lewis Hine's photographs framing the soaring angles of the Empire State Building as it rose under the feet of the high steel workers, and Margaret Bourke-White celebrating steel and concrete in her silvery prints.

Natan's first drawing in the series must be the one of the 55th Street site before any work had begun. Looking down from a high point, there is an array

of rooftops: lines and angles, anonymous and static. Nothing's happening, or if anything is, it's hidden behind the walls of the buildings. The pictures that follow are familiar scenes of streets I've walked down a hundred times. I know where I am.

The next drawings show the excavation, and suddenly things begin to come to life. There is sky, space, and light: we're below street level, looking up. Strange shapes turn into familiar things: a soaring cliff turns out to be the wall of the next-door building. Our neighbor's backyard is exposed, revealing a tree, a utility ladder, and a telephone pole.

Then the machines arrive. They are mammoth! Even so, the wheels in their tracks and their enormous, jointed arms seem small surrounded by

Many, like Lester, a drill man, or Richard, a foreman, have very serious expressions: they are proud of their work and committed to doing a good job.

towering Manhattan office buildings. Now and then there is a human-size detail in these drawings—a hammer resting on top of some lumber or a worker on scaffolding on the far side of the excavation—that reminds me, with a jolt, of the giant scale of this project.

The drawings verge on the abstract, emphasizing the wheel of a giant digging machine, the perfect curve of a worker's hard hat, or the straight lines of supporting poles, with their angled shadows against the concrete foundation. These details gleam against the deep-charcoal background of the hole.

The diggers, steel-workers, drivers, and carpenters come into the pictures: they're reaching out over the scaffolding, handling a welding torch, pouring concrete. Now I see

that it's more than just a big hole in the ground. The work being done here will literally support us as we all climb up toward the sky.

So many of these things that are common sights in the city—trucks, cranes, shrouded scaffolds, steel beams—in the drawings are shapes and forms playing together, as light and dark and energy. I love the way our neighbor's tree, a vestige of real life, insists on popping back into the picture, reminding us of its existence.

Natan did more than chronicle the birth of a new building; he captured the people who made it. Right from the start he snapped portraits of the workers, transformed these into drawings, and bestowed them as gifts to the subjects.

There's nothing abstract about these portraits. Each one tells me something about the person's life, his skill, his contribution. Many, like Lester, a drill man, or Richard, a foreman, have very serious expressions: they are proud of their work and committed to doing a good job. Many are smiling. Some, like Freddy, a drilling specialist, or Dan, an ironworker, seem to be having a great day. And why not? Our magnificent building is going up! Why shouldn't our spirits be lifted in the process? I'm glad we have a record of those moments.

The building is complete. We occupied it in November 2004. Nicky, Dave, Kevin, Jon, Lea, Gildo, and Ralph, and the other workers have long since moved on to other jobs on other buildings, but we remember them through Natan's pictures. Their efforts are subsumed

in the present tense —Chaya, Clifton, Matthew, Asha, Renee, Dwana, and I, along with so many others, have taken their places, adding music and movement to the layers of history and memory that also dwell here.

I wanted to bring Mr. Ailey with us to our new home. Often, when I'm in the building, I go from the bottom to the top floor— eight stories in all! —greeting everyone I see, keeping the flow going. "What's up? What's going on?" I say, knowing there will always be so much going on in this wonderful place. This building is Mr. Ailey's legacy, brought to reality by Natan, Carolyn, and a great team of people, many of whom are represented in Natan's drawings. His work serves as a tribute both to the structure and to the idea; the pictures reveal to us how we got here, and we won't forget.

—JUDITH JAMISON

Building
Ailey

RICHARD BENA
Foreman

CLIFTON WHITE
Security

LESTER CHATMAN
Drill man

"In its iconic architecture, Ailey's new home lifts its dancers to amazing city views, as if Manhattan had a mountaintop"

—SUSAN CHIN, *FAIA*, New York City Department of Cultural Affairs

The site as seen from high above

"Following an intensive two-year search, we signed the 100-page contract of sale with WNET for the acquisition of the United Studio Building at 851 Ninth Avenue. For the first time I knew with certainty that those who said, 'This will never happen; you are wasting your time,' were wrong: the dream would be realized."

—ARTHUR J. MIRANTE, Cushman & Wakefield,
   building committee board member, Alvin Ailey American Dance Theater

View of the old theater, looking east

The old WNET theater

An old theater makes room for dance

FREDDY
Drill man

JOEY
Operations engineer

FRANKLIN
Drill runner's assistant

"Even before the property at 55th and Ninth Avenue had been selected, I was afforded the opportunity to assist Alvin Ailey in the arena of governmental relations and advocacy. Working with the Alvin Ailey team, I served as an interpreter, explaining how and why government had a say-so in the design and construction of the first home for Ailey and working to secure significant public funding and approvals for the project. We listened to the community members' critique of the design. Working with the team as Natan revised the design to secure the needed approvals made me feel a part of the Ailey family."

—CLAUDIA WAGNER, law offices of Claudia Wagner LLC

Excavation along the garage building; the hardest rock

Shoring: providing a
stable foundation to the
building north of Ailey

BRUCE PHILLIP
Assistant project
manager

JIMMY
Excavation

TOMMY
Drill man

KEVIN
Carpenter

MICHAEL
Shop steward

JORGE
Carpenter

Shoring the 55th
Street side

Drilling and breaking rock

Shoring the sidewalk

Jim Christerson,
associate partner,
Iu + Bibliowcz, on a
rainy day observing
the unstable building
to the north

"Looking into the excavation on a rainy day, I remember worrying about water and foundations– mortal enemies. And I realized that this was it. We were all committed to bringing the building out of the ground and making it a wonderful place for dance."

—JIM CHRISTERSON, *associate partner, Iu + Bibliowicz Architects*

Excavating 26 feet to house the black-box theater

GEORGE KALOGEROPAULOS
Electrical engineer

ANGELA BILLINGHURST
Equal opportunity administrator

NICK
Laborer

The tree and
the pole

KENETH BROWN
Traffic control

DAVE LEDGISTER
Laborer

BOB GRAVES
Ironworker

The Hitachi crane
forever present
during excavation

"This was a particularly challenging project because you had to meet the very unique and varied requirements of the Alvin Ailey American Dance Theater as well as the expectations and vision of the various trustees and major donors. All this while balancing artistic creativity with the realities of construction costs and schedules."

—ANTHONY M. CARVETTE, Structuretone,
  building committee board member, Alvin Ailey American Dance Theater

Drilling along the
parking garage
west of the site

Continuing to
excavate as the
residential building
across the street
continues to grow

DAN JACOBS
Ironworker

RICKEY GORDON
Ironworker

DANNY DOYLE
Ironworker

JOHN HATTEN
Ironworker

As Gotham, the building across the street, goes up, Ailey digs down

Concrete for our foundation walls

"I remember the Monday morning in October when the final phase of demolishing the existing building came to a halt. There, exposed before us, was the adjacent neighbor's exterior wall, which had been erected over the past year. We dared not continue for fear this recent addition would come tumbling down. We contacted the Department of Buildings about what we believed to be poor construction that did not appear to meet any codes, only to be informed that we would have to resolve this issue on our own. The sketch represents the solution we used to permanently create an external steel skeleton that could be anchored to our foundation wall with temporary diagonal braces to stabilize the building from the future excavation and construction we had ahead of us."

—JULIO A. VILLAVICENCIO, *project manager,* Jones Lang Lasalle

Steel supports
stabilize the
neighboring
building

Steel supports

The unstable building

Excavating around the bracing

"When we installed the curtain wall on the studio walls, especially the fifth floor studio at the southeast corner of the building, it was at that moment I realized just how beautiful those upper studios were going to be–the light, the views, the transparency between outside and inside. It made me (almost) wish I was a dancer and could just dance in that space. It was like they were going to float above the street."

—NANCY CZESAK, *project manager,* Tishman Construction

Gotham's crane

STEVE FALCO
Ironworker

VICTOR TRETYAKOV
Security consultant

JOHN CIVETTA
Excavation

CHRIS ALTANER
Truck driver

KARL LEE
Project manager

JOE FERNANDES
Maintenance

Watchful eye of Jon Lyons, project superintendent

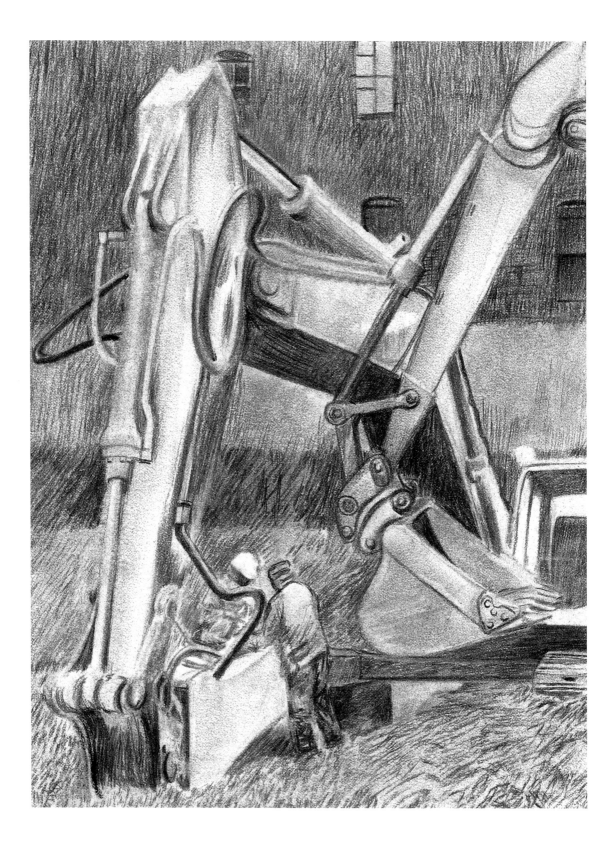

"It was August 14th at 4:20 P.M. I was driving home from the site, all the delays were behind us, and we were finally flying with the foundation walls when the radio station stopped playing. I switched stations, but nothing happened. I looked in the rearview mirror expecting to see smoke coming from Manhattan. Nothing. Turns out, there was a power outage on the Eastern Seaboard. *Great,* I thought, *forms are set, and 80 yards of concrete are ordered for 8:00 A.M. Another delay.* I thought the project was jinxed. I went to the city at about 5:00 A.M. —no building lights, no traffic lights. People were driving like the world was ending. I got to the site, and to my surprise more than half the crew was there. Everyone looked to me for direction. The first crisis was hot coffee. There was a rumor that a small strip of the Bronx had power, so we sent up a laborer. Were we going to let a small thing like no power stop us? We repeated our mantra: 'Nothing stops concrete.' We contacted the plant: They had generators, so we had generators–it was a go. We were the only job in the city that poured that day. Anything to maintain the schedule."

—JON LYONS, *project superintendant,* Tishman Construction

Excavation was delayed because of the unstable building to the north of the Ailey site. Jon Lyons, project superintendent, had brought his son to the site. The boy made a very pointed observation to his dad, suggesting he should switch construction companies, as the Gotham building south of us was progressing so much faster than ours, even though it started excavating after we did. Little did his son know that our hopes to catch up and make up for lost time were in his dad's hands.

—NATAN BIBLIOWCZ

Hammer drill breaking the rock

Rock removal

View looking west

Pouring concrete for the foundation

JEFF AXEL
Assistant project manager

GARY COHEN
Project manager

RUDY
Ironworker

"It was very fulfilling to work on a project that will leave its mark in dance history and give back to the community and the arts for many years to come."

—JEFFERY AXEL, *assistant project manager,* Tishman Construction

Attaching reinforcing steel bars for the foundation walls

A view east

Wood forms being installed

More concrete arriving

Rock shadows

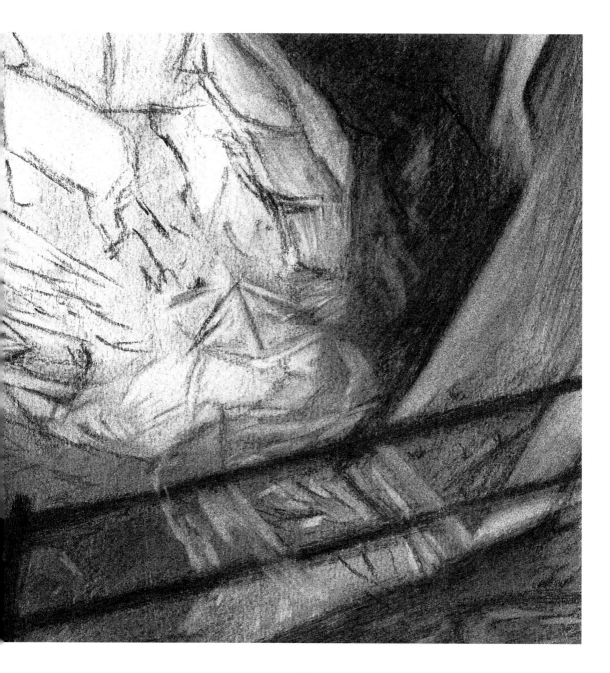

Pouring concrete for
the foundation walls

Foundation walls
with waterproofing,
forms sitting idle

"One fine Saturday morning in the spring, I was walking down 55th Street with my husband and four-year-old son. We were on our way to see the *Queen Mary 2,* which was docked at Pier 92. I wanted to take them past the Ailey site. The walls were rising up into the air. I pointed to the building and said, 'See, this is Mommy's new work.' My son was impressed. As I watched them looking at the building and taking pictures, I realized that this was something that would last far beyond us."

—PAM ROBINSON, *director of finance and administration,* Alvin Ailey American Dance Theater

North foundation
wall, tree, ladder,
and telephone pole

Waterproofing the
foundation wall of
the black−box theater

Construction sheds on Ninth Avenue

RALPH
Electrician

SAL MASSARO
Electrician

In the shoring pit

"Natan and I have collaborated on many projects, but the Ailey building is special. More than any other project we have worked on, this one was driven by the passion of the entire Ailey organization, from board members to the dancers, to make a dream come true. Our studio wanted to create something special that would realize that dream. And it was the passion of the construction team, with whom we interacted every day. We worked together as a team, and it was the experience of a lifetime."

—CAROLYN IU, *partner,* Iu + Bibliowicz Architects

Northeast corner

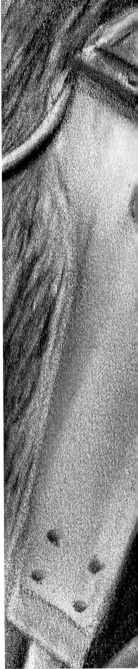

Cleaning the
concrete bucket

Gildo Panagussi making his rounds

Installing reinforcing mesh
along the sidewalk foundation wall

Preparing forms to
complete the foundation

NATHAN
Electrician

GILDO PANAGUSSI
Super excavation and foundation

PETERIS RATAS
Architect, Iu + Bibliowicz
Architects

Building wood forms

The site of the
black−box theater and
tap−dancing studios

Making the precast stair at the Castcon plant in Pittsburgh

Pouring concrete for the precast stairs at the Pittsburg plant

Gary Cohen

Nate
10/03

PABLO BRUNO
Structural engineer

CLIFF
Ironworker

HENRY MCGEE
Board member

Welding steel plates
along foundation walls

North foundation wall

Our friends, the excavators and the foundation contractors, are gone —N.B.

"It was our goal to have the structure fit seamlessly within the architectural character of the building."

—PHILIP MURRAY, *partner and structural engineer,* Gilsanz Murray Steficek

Securing the steel beams

"Designing the mechanical and
electrical systems for the Alvin Ailey
building underscored the importance of
incorporating the varying requirements
for the dance studios, the black–box theater,
and the administrative offices in order
to create the proper thermal, acoustical,
and lighting environment for each of
these portions of the project."
—DON MONGITORE, *partner,* Jaros, Baum & Bolles

Steel moves up. Worker welds metal deck to steel beams

Steel rising

"I couldn't wait for the building to be finished. Coming to 55th Street gave me the sense that we were moving forward. The new building is so filled with energy that it gives the choreographer, creative artists, and dancers a sense that this is a great place to live, grow, and create. The building has so much life."

—MASAZUMI CHAYA, *associate artistic director,* Alvin Ailey American Dance Theater

LAILA
Electrician

PAUL KRAMER
Project manager

LAURA HUCH
Precast concrete

Ground–floor
steel, as seen
from below

Fifth floor; almost no sight of our neighbor

Looking west

The roof davits for
the screens and
steel supports for
the mechanical
equipment, looking
through elevator
machine room

Billowing drapes as the
building is fireproofed

"I take great pride in 'walking jobs.' There is
something about all the hard hats, the smell
of drywall, dust, wet concrete, and fresh paint
that says to me things are really coming together.
That cold morning in November, when I started
at the top and walked down, I witnessed all
the chapters of the Ailey building's birth. We
were finishing offices on the top while concrete
slabs were being poured in the lobby. Would
it ever get done? It always does!"

—DAN TISHMAN, Tishman Construction

Christo–esque
fireproofing steel

"As I stood watching the Ailey dancers test the sprung–flooring mock-up by jumping and spinning, the connection between those dancers and the hours I spent in the design studio and on the construction site really became clear. I felt like part of the Ailey family. I still feel the connection every time I see a performance or a poster on the sidewalk or when I walk by the building."

—DARIN REYNOLDS, *associate,* Iu + Bibliowicz Architects

Last piece of
curtain wall
being installed

Elevator shaft

"Although I have been involved in the design and construction of many projects, this one is a particularly fascinating collaboration of artists working together in various media. It was a wonderful experience to see the architects, dancers, artistic directors, board members, project managers, and builders contribute their specialized talents to a carefully orchestrated process in which the full potential of the project's vision was realized. Everyone involved in the process now feels a sense of pride in the success of this unusual artistic collaboration."

—KATHERINE FARLEY, Tishman Construction, *board member*, Alvin Ailey American Dance Theater

Waterproofing the
inner courtyard

The acoustic panels for the
dance studios being lowered
into place. These panels
allowed the black−box
theater to be divided into
two dance studios

Curtain wall being
installed up from
the second floor

View looking west,
with roof screens

The building begins
to glow at the edge
of the marquee

Building the Alvin Ailey American Dance Theater was a labor of love for so many. The subjects I was able to draw made me feel more connected to them and helped me to better understand the camaraderie among these skilled people in a variety of trades. I thank them all for what they did to complete this great dance institution. —N.B.

DAVID BIBLIOWICZ

ANCE THEATER

"The project team was
constantly motivated
to perform at the highest
level of collaboration,
professionalism, and
goal–oriented service
delivery, knowing that
we were building a home
for a world–class artistic
organization."
—DAVID N. HOROWITZ,
project executive, Jones Lang Lasalle

"At the start of construction, I visited the site every week, and by the end I was there every day. However, it was many weeks after we had actually moved in that I walked along Ninth Avenue, looked up, and really saw the building for the first time. With the Ailey banners and dance pictures in the window, it was then that I realized we had truly arrived!"

—SHARON GERSTEN LUCKMAN, *executive director,*
Alvin Ailey American Dance Theater

Bio

NATAN BIBLIOWICZ
Architect

Natan Bibliowicz, born in Colombia and raised in Peru, graduated from Cornell University in 1981. In 1999, he and Carolyn Iu formed the architectural firm Iu + Bibliowicz Architects, whose wide range of projects include hotels in Asia, corporate headquarters, high-end residential projects, community centers, high-rise office portfolios, and performing arts venues all over the United States. The firm designed the Alvin Ailey American Dance Theater, in New York City. The building opened in the spring of 2005.

Natan had practiced architecture at Skidmore Owings & Merrill and Kohn Pedersen & Fox ealry in his career.

Bibliowicz lives in New York City and Harrison, New York with his wife, Jessica, and two sons, Tommy and David.